NAMES *of* GOD
Glimpses of *His Character*

8 studies
for individuals or groups

Douglas Connelly

With Notes for Leaders

D1407526

Scripture Union is an international Christian charity working with churches in more than 130 countries.

Thank you for purchasing this book. Any profits from this book support SU in England and Wales to bring the good news of Jesus Christ to children, young people and families and to enable them to meet God through the Bible and prayer.

Find out more about our work and how you can get involved at:

www.scriptureunion.org.uk (England and Wales)
www.suscotland.org.uk (Scotland)
www.suni.co.uk (Northern Ireland)
www.scriptureunion.org (USA)
www.su.org.au (Australia)

ISBN 978 1 84427 725 4

First published in the United States by InterVarsity Press 2012.
Published in Great Britain by Scripture Union 2012.

British Library Cataloguing-in-Publication data: a catalogue record for this book is available from the British Library.

Printed in India by Thomson Press India Ltd.

Contents

Getting the Most Out of
Names of God

For most of us, our names simply identify us. We might be named in honor of a grandmother or some famous person, but our names don't have much meaning or significance beyond that. This is not the case, however, with the names given to God in the Bible. God's names and titles are windows into his character. We learn about who God is and what God is ready to do in our lives by coming to understand his names.

To be precise, God has only one name. In the Old Testament, the one true and living God reveals himself as "the LORD." But God is also given a variety of descriptive titles in Scripture. These "names" help us see more deeply into God's nature and work and power.

This study guide is an exploration of the key "names of God" revealed in the Bible. But it's not just an academic study centered on ancient words and obscure events. Each study is designed to give you a clearer understanding of who God is and draw you closer to God in worship and devotion and trust.

The God who revealed himself to Moses and to Abraham is the same God we relate to today. We have come to know him as God the Father and as Jesus the Savior and as the Spirit of holiness—but he is also the LORD Almighty, the God who provides, the God of glory.

So be prepared to have your heart and mind stirred as you explore God's nature in greater depth—and be prepared to have your life and worship changed by these encounters with the living God!

Suggestions for Individual Study

1. As you begin each study, pray that God will speak to you through his Word.

2. Read the introduction to the study and respond to the personal reflection question or exercise. This is designed to help you focus on God and on the theme of the study.

3. Each study deals with a particular passage so that you can delve into the author's meaning in that context. Read and re-read the passage to be studied. The questions are written using the language of the New International Version, so you may wish to use that version of the Bible. The New Revised Standard Version is also recommended.

4. This is an inductive Bible study, designed to help you discover for yourself what Scripture is saying. The study includes three types of questions. *Observation* questions ask about the basic facts: who, what, when, where and how. *Interpretation* questions delve into the meaning of the passage. *Application* questions help you discover the implications of the text for growing in Christ. These three keys unlock the treasures of Scripture.

Write your answers to the questions in the spaces provided or in a personal journal. Writing can bring clarity and deeper understanding of yourself and of God's Word.

5. It might be good to have a Bible dictionary handy. Use it to look up any unfamiliar words, names or places.

6. Use the prayer suggestion to guide you in thanking God for what you have learned and to pray about the applications that have come to mind.

7. You may want to go on to the suggestion under "Now or Later," or you may want to use that idea for your next study.

Suggestions for Members of a Group Study

1. Come to the study prepared. Follow the suggestions for individual study mentioned above. You will find that careful preparation will greatly enrich your time spent in group discussion.

2. Be willing to participate in the discussion. The leader of your group will not be lecturing. Instead, he or she will be encouraging the members of the group to discuss what they have learned. The leader will be asking the questions that are found in this guide.

3. Stick to the topic being discussed. Your answers should be based on the verses which are the focus of the discussion and not on outside authorities such as commentaries or speakers. These studies focus on a particular passage of Scripture. Only rarely should you refer to other portions of the Bible. This allows for everyone to participate in in-depth study on equal ground.

4. Be sensitive to the other members of the group. Listen attentively when they describe what they have learned. You may be surprised by their insights! Each question assumes a variety of answers. Many questions do not have "right" answers, particularly questions that aim at meaning or application. Instead the questions push us to explore the passage more thoroughly.

When possible, link what you say to the comments of others. Also, be affirming whenever you can. This will encourage some of the more hesitant members of the group to participate.

5. Be careful not to dominate the discussion. We are sometimes so eager to express our thoughts that we leave too little opportunity for others to respond. By all means participate! But allow others to also.

6. Expect God to teach you through the passage being discussed and through the other members of the group. Pray that you will have an enjoyable and profitable time together, but also that as a result of the study you will find ways that you can take action individually and/or as a group.

7. Remember that anything said in the group is considered confidential and should not be discussed outside the group unless specific permission is given to do so.

8. If you are the group leader, you will find additional suggestions at the back of the guide.

1

One Supreme Being

"I don't believe in God—never have, never will!" The words came casually from the young man's lips.

"Why?" I asked in return. "What's your reason for rejecting God's existence?"

"I don't know," he said after a moment's hesitation. "I guess I've never seen anything to convince me that God is really there. God may exist, I guess, but he doesn't care about me."

GROUP DISCUSSION. Why do you believe God exists?

PERSONAL REFLECTION. How do you usually respond when someone denies or doubts the existence of God? What can you do to develop an even more inviting and engaging response?

The writers of the Bible never set out to prove the existence of God. They just declare that he is—and that he is personally involved with the world and the people he has made. In the first verse of the Bible we come face to face with Elohim, the awesome God of creation. *Read Genesis 1.*

1. Go back through the passage and underline or note every occurrence of the word "God." What activities is God said to do?

He speaks   He gives
He creates   He sees
He Blesses   He instructs

Do those actions point to a personal being or an impersonal force? Explain.

Personal - He cares & relates to His creation (what He has created)

2. What is the significance of the order of creation?

Everything needed was a place before Man was created.

What does that order convey about the place of human beings in God's creation?

We are high in God's eyes than We think do

We need to go beyond our comfort zone, recognizing our own smallness, to appreciate fully the mystery & majesty of God's creation.

3. The Hebrew word translated "God" here is *Elohim*, which speaks of God as the one eternal being, the majestic, powerful Creator. Everyone and everything else had a beginning, but God has always existed. As our passage reveals, when the eternal God speaks, things happen. What does this fact convey to you about God's power?

His power has no limit
He is supreme Creator

4. Into what situation in your life would you like God to speak with his creative power?

What difference would it make?

5. God evaluates each stage of his creation (vv. 4, 10, 12, 18, 21, 25, 31). What insight into God's character can you grasp from his evaluation?

God saw "that it was good"
His goodness & His mercy

How does God's evaluation influence your own view of the created world and your responsibility toward it?

Without worshipping creation, as some do, we
need to respect and care for what God has
created.

6. What role does God give human beings in this newly created world (vv. 26, 28)?

We are stewards of it, we have a god-given
responsibility to care.

How well are humans fulfilling that role today?

not always very well!

7. What does it mean for you to be created in God's image (v. 27)?

I am the daughter - He is my father.

How does that fact affect how you view and relate to other people?

They too are made in the image of God & we want non-christians to see Jesus in us

---

8. What do you think the appropriate responses of human beings should be toward their Creator God?

One of awe & of Glorifying

How can you weave those responses into your daily routine?

In prayer & by being responsible

Acknowledge God as your Creator and the bestower of all good gifts. Express your adoration of him in words of praise and thanks.

Now or Later

When David contemplated the magnitude of God's creation, he was struck by how insignificant one human being is. Read Psalm 8 and then walk outside on a clear night and look into the heavens. Let yourself be awed by the majesty of a God who could bring such marvels into existence by the power of his word alone.

If this study prompts a desire to be a better steward of creation, check out some websites that explore this issue. If you search "creation care" on the Internet, you will find several Christian organizations that can provide direction for caring for your slice of God's creation.

2

God Most High

I talked today with a man who hasn't been in church for twenty years. At one time he attended services regularly and even participated in the leadership of a congregation. "Why did you quit?" I asked.

His answer was one I had heard before. "I just didn't get anything out of it. I got bored and haven't been back."

It's difficult even for committed Christians to remember that genuine worship isn't really about *getting;* it's far more about *giving.* We give God our praise and adoration; we give our time and money and energy in honor of the Lord and in thanks for his goodness; we give ourselves in ministry and service to others. And when we give freely and sacrificially, an amazing thing happens. Our needs are met too, and we receive an abundance of blessing from God.

GROUP DISCUSSION. Explain what is hardest for you to "give" in worship—and why you might find it so difficult.

PERSONAL REFLECTION. Think about your most recent worship experience. Where was your attention: on yourself, on others or on the Lord? How can you be more intentional and focused in your worship?

When Abram heard that a group of enemies had attacked the city of Sodom and had captured his nephew Lot he knew something had to be done, and done quickly. So Abram gathered a small army of trusted friends and servants from his own household and pursued the attackers. In a stunning victory, he recovered everything that was plundered and every captive that was taken. A representative of El Elyon, God Most High, met Abram as he returned in triumph. He fell down in worship before the God of such power and mercy. *Read Genesis 14:17-24.*

---

1. What questions would you like to ask Abram about his encounter with Melchizedek?

What questions would you like to ask Melchizedek?

---

2. Melchizedek is called both a king and a priest. How does Melchizedek fulfill each role in this scene?

---

3. Go back through the text and mark the four occurrences of the title "God Most High." What does this name convey to you about God's character and actions?

4. What does the fact that God is "God Most High" mean as you think about your personal life (career, relationships, decisions, etc.)?

5. What was the significance of the tenth that Abram gave to Melchizedek (v. 20)?

6. Why did Abram refuse the offer of the king of Sodom to keep all the goods that he had recaptured?

7. When do you think Abram took the oath before God—before he pursued the enemy kings or after?

Why is that significant?

8. What does Abram's oath say about his relationship with God Most High?

9. How might Abram have lived differently after this experience?

10. What would be appropriate responses for you to make to God Most High?

How can you incorporate those responses into your worship and daily activities?

Ask God to give you a deeper sense of his majestic reign as sovereign King—and a willingness to submit your own heart to his authority.

Now or Later

David wrote Psalm 7 in response to an attack on his character and reputation by an enemy. He asks God "Most High" to rise up in his defense (Psalm 7:8) and promises to sing praise to "the LORD Most High" when he is delivered by God's power (Psalm 7:17). Read Psalm 7 or compose your own song of praise to God as the one who rules over our world and over our lives in sovereign authority. Encourage someone who may feel attacked by sharing the truth that God has not forgotten us or lost control of his world. He still reigns as God Most High.

3

God's Personal Name

The "names" of God that we find in the Bible are more accurately referred to as descriptive titles. Really God has only one name. His personal name, the name he has revealed to his people, is Yahweh (or, in older versions of the Bible, Jehovah). The name Yahweh speaks of God's eternal existence and his unchanging character. He is the "I AM" (which is what *Yahweh* means in Hebrew). Our God stands above the past, present and future as the ever-present Lord of all.

Yahweh occurs 6,823 times in the Old Testament. In the Hebrew language, Yahweh is written with only four consonants and no vowels: YHWH. The name was considered so holy that for hundreds of years Jewish people would not even pronounce the word. When they came to YHWH in the Bible, they would say the word Adonai instead, which means "Lord" or "Master." YHWH is translated "LORD" in most English versions, as in Isaiah 42:8: "I am the LORD; that is my name!"

GROUP DISCUSSION. What "name" do you use most often when you talk to God in prayer? What does that name convey to your mind and heart?

PERSONAL REFLECTION. How does it make you feel to hear God's name used in a vulgar or flippant way? What is your attitude toward God when you call on him by name?

Psalm 68 was probably first sung when King David was bring-
ing the ark of the covenant into the city of Jerusalem in preparation for the building of the great temple by David's son Solomon (2 Samuel 6:12-18). A choir would have sung the psalm's
stanzas, which review God's mighty deeds for his people, Israel.
It's a stirring shout of praise for the victory of God over all his
enemies. What makes this psalm so unique is the variety of
names and titles for God that are used. The word "God" (Elohim) can be found twenty-three times, along with Yahweh, Yah
(a shortened form of Yahweh), Adonai and Shaddai (Almighty).
David's words help us even today to exalt the name and the
nature of our God! *Read Psalm 68:1-20.*

---

1. The psalm surveys in poetic fashion God's mighty works.
Looking back through verses 1-20, underline the names and
descriptive titles for God that you find. Which name is the most
familiar to you and why?

Which name is the most unfamiliar?

2. David highlights some of God's greatest deeds. Which verses point to

a. God's deliverance of Israel from slavery in Egypt?

   v 7,8

b. God's provision and protection of his people in the wilderness journey?

c. God's assistance in defeating the rulers of Canaan, the land of promise?

d. God's continuing care for his people today?

   v 10

What thoughts about God would this review of the past stir in the hearts of the worshipers as the ark of the covenant drew near the city of Jerusalem?

---

3. Give a brief review of God's mighty works in your life from when he rescued you from sin's slavery to his care for you through life's journey.

4. David specifically focuses on "the LORD" in verses 4-6. What aspects of God's character does he emphasize?

Eternal God.

Which one of those qualities of God means the most to you right now and why?

5. What areas of your life feel like high "mountains" (v. 15) or barren "wastelands" (v. 7)?

6. What would change in those situations if the LORD came to you as one who shakes the earth (vv. 7-8)?

What would it mean if he came as one who brings gentle rain (vv. 8-9)?

7. The "chariots of God" are most likely a reference to God's angels (v. 17). The LORD's greatness is revealed by the vast army of powerful angels who accompany him. How do you feel when you think about warrior angels protecting you as a child of God? Safe? Intimidated? Explain your answer.

8. List the benefits that come to those who trust in the LORD (vv. 19-20). He is our Saviour

He bears our burdens

He saves us, from death.

9. Which of those benefits most encourages you?

Which can you share with a friend who is having a difficult time?

10. Based on what you have learned in this psalm about the LORD, what responses from you are appropriate and worthy of his name?

Use the different names and titles of God from this psalm to praise him for his blessings and protection over you.

Now or Later

The New Testament applies verse 18 of this psalm to Jesus and his triumph over his enemies. Read Ephesians 4:8-13. The one change Paul makes in this verse is that, rather than *receiving* gifts from conquered kings, Jesus *gives* the trophies of his victory to the church. What are the "gifts" Jesus gives? How can you reflect that fact in your attitude toward those people whom Paul says are given to the church?

4

The God
Who Provides

Genesis 22:1-14

The van was empty. We had carried all my daughter's clothes and gear up to her dorm room. After we hugged, she turned to head back across campus to a new season in her life. Before I had the van out of the parking lot, tears were streaming down my face. I was leaving a child of my own flesh behind. It was only for a semester at college, but the pain of separation stirred up my emotions.

GROUP DISCUSSION. Describe a painful separation in your life. Was it temporary or permanent? Who or what helped you during that time?

PERSONAL REFLECTION. What relationship of yours would be most difficult to lose? How would you feel if God asked you to leave the person you cared about most?

God had promised Abraham that he would have more descendants than the stars in the sky. And so, even though Abraham's wife Sarah was barren and Abraham and Sarah were getting on in years, God gave them a son. Isaac was conceived and born as a demonstration of God's power. Now God would make a staggering request of Abraham—and would once again show himself to be a God who comes to the rescue when all hope is lost. *Read Genesis 22:1-14.*

1. As you scan back through the account, what bothers you most about what happened?

2. Describe Abraham's response to God (vv. 2-3).

What does his response reveal about his relationship with God?

3. In what areas do you think God is testing your faith right now?

How are you responding to the test?

4. Do you think Abraham would actually have killed Isaac? Explain your answer.

5. Why are Abraham's words to his servants in verse 5 significant?

6. For whose benefit does God wait until the very last moment to stop Abraham? His own? Abraham's? Isaac's? Ours? Explain your answer.

7. God provided a ram as the substitute sacrifice for Isaac, so Abraham named the place "The LORD Will Provide" (in Hebrew, Yahweh-yireh). What does that name communicate to you about the character of Abraham's God?

How does knowing God as the Provider encourage you in your present life circumstances?

8. What or who is the "Isaac" in your life—the most prized person or entity, and the focus of your life?

---

9. Are you willing to place your Isaac on the altar before God and give it over completely to him?

What can you be confident about if you do?

Be prepared to praise God whether he restores your "Isaac" or removes it. God can be trusted to provide for every need.

Now or Later

God did not ask Abraham to do something that God himself was not willing to do. God willingly sacrificed his own Son. How far did God go in that sacrifice? Think about how Jesus was like Isaac. Then think about how Jesus was like the ram as our substitute on the cross. Express your thankfulness to Jesus in prayer or in song for bearing our sin and guilt on the cross.

5

The LORD Almighty

1 Samuel 17:1-51

The man sitting in my office was broken—and broke. He had lost his house, his business, his family and his reputation. His gambling addiction had become all-consuming. What made it worse was that he didn't see the problem. Everyone else saw the wicked "giant" in his life, but he refused to acknowledge its presence. He was convinced that he just needed that one big score to win back everything he had lost.

What the man needed was a new source of power in his life! His own resources were exhausted, and he had no ability in himself to turn away from the things that were destroying him. My counsel to him was to begin to rely on the God of power, the God able to do what he could not do, the God who could supply the strength that he lacked.

We all find ourselves in places of weakness at times. Our hope and confidence when we are coming up short are in the LORD Almighty, the God of strength.

GROUP DISCUSSION. What are some of the giants that you have seen in other people's lives—intimidating spouses or overwhelming circumstances or addictive behaviors that seemed to take control? How did those people handle the powerful forces? Stand and fight? Run and hide? Live in denial?

PERSONAL REFLECTION. What are the giants in your life? How have you tried to handle them up to this point? How successful have you been?

David had learned even as a very young man to face enemies with courage and with trust in God. When a lion or a bear threatened his father's sheep, David went after it and made sure it never harmed the sheep again. When David heard the threats of a Philistine thug against God's people, David determined to follow the same course of action. *Read 1 Samuel 17:1-51.*

1. The author of 1 Samuel tells us a lot about Goliath (vv. 4-7). What does all the detail convey to you about this enemy?

2. What rewards did Saul offer to try to motivate a champion from Israel to fight Goliath (v. 25)?

3. What motivated David to accept the challenge (vv. 26, 36-37)?

4. Is your attitude toward the intimidating giants in your life more like David's (v. 37) or more like Saul's (v. 11)? Explain or give an example of your answer.

5. Circle David's references to "the LORD Almighty" in this passage. What does the description "Almighty" say to you about who God is and what kind of resource he can be in your life?

6. What fears do you struggle with when you turn and face the enemy that defies God and seeks to defeat you?

7. How would those fears change if you were fully confident that God was on your side?

8. What did David predict would be the end result of the battle for Goliath (vv. 45-47)?

What would be the larger purpose of the battle for Israel and for the world (vv. 46-47)?

9. What might be some of the larger purposes for the battles you face—for your family or circle of friends or coworkers?

---

10. What was David's role in the battle?

---

11. What specifically do you need God to supply in your battle with life's giants?

What will you bring to the battle?

Ask God to bring his power into the difficult situations you are facing—and then offer up whatever you can bring for his use. Now turn and face the enemy in the power of the LORD Almighty.

Now or Later

Talk as a group or think about some of the "Goliath" issues in our culture—issues that defy God and taunt his people. Brainstorm ways you as a small group or as an individual, unarmed and relatively weak, might help to bring those giants down. Read Psalm 66:1-7 as an encouraging conclusion to your session.

6

Holy, Holy God

It was not a day I had been looking forward to. I had the responsibility of confronting two men with serious wrong in their lives. My part went pretty much the same in both meetings. I laid out the situation gently but firmly, and pleaded with each man to repent and turn away from the paths they were on. I promised them God's forgiveness if they would respond correctly.

The difference in the two meetings was the response. The first man was broken in sorrow and repentance. The tears started flowing just seconds after I started talking. We ended the meeting by embracing and committing to walk through the consequences together.

The second man had no tears. He stiffened when I began to talk and chose the path of anger and self-justification. He left without an embrace or a prayer. I probably won't see him again. Same issues, same confrontation, very different responses.

GROUP DISCUSSION. When you were younger, what were the issues that prompted you to "rebel" against your parents or teachers? What punishments or reprimands were handed out? Tell one story to the group.

PERSONAL REFLECTION. What are the issues that prompt a rebellious spirit in you toward God? How do you typically respond to his correction in your life?

Isaiah is one of the most revered prophets in the Bible. He had a long and faithful ministry to the people of Judah. But when God called Isaiah to be his spokesman, Isaiah was overwhelmed with a stunning sense of his own sinfulness. He started, however, where we all need to start—he turned in repentance to God and received cleansing and forgiveness from God's holy hand. Then Isaiah set out on a ministry of confronting God's people with their sin and dispensing God's comfort as they faced the consequences of their failure. *Read Isaiah 1:1-20.*

1. If you look at this passage as a court scene, who are the witnesses and who is the judge (v. 2)?

Who is being prosecuted and what are the charges (vv. 3-4)?

2. How would you summarize the spiritual condition of the people?

3. Do you see any parallels to our present-day culture? Explain.

4. Why does God reject the worship the people of Judah offer him (vv. 10-14)?

5. Do you think God could say similar things to the church today? Explain your answer.

6. How does God's holy character influence his response to prayer (vv. 15-16)?

7. God prescribes negative and positive correction in the lives of the people of Judah (vv. 16-17). Make a list of both aspects and describe what obedience to each might look like in your life.

8. What is significant about God's promises of forgiveness and cleansing (vv. 18-19)?

9. Isaiah uses the title "the Holy One of Israel" (v. 4) twenty-nine times in his book. What does it mean to you that God is holy?

10. In what specific ways does God's holy character prompt holy living in you?

Pray that God will continue to build his holy character in your life.

Now or Later

Isaiah links personal holiness with the pursuit of social justice. What issues of justice and morality in our culture are you interested in? Commit to becoming more deeply involved in one of those issues and to better informing your family and friends about it.

7

The God of Glory

Psalm 29

I love thunderstorms! When the thunder starts rumbling at night, I actually get up to watch the lightning flash and listen to the wind blow. I even have a CD called *Wilderness Thunderstorm* that I play once in a while in my office. The sights and sounds of a storm demonstrate the power and majesty of God to me.

One of the most memorable storms I've experienced swept across the central Pennsylvania mountains late one summer evening when I was about twelve years old. I watched it from the upstairs window of my grandparents' house (with the window open, of course). The wind whipped the curtains around my head and the thunder rattled the glass. Finally the rain began to fall in big drops and the smell of the freshly washed air filled the room.

GROUP DISCUSSION. What natural events reveal God's power and glory most dramatically to you? Tell the group about a time you personally witnessed such an event.

PERSONAL REFLECTION. In what setting do you most clearly sense the presence of God—in a majestic cathedral, out in the wilderness, listening to children play? How do you respond to God when you feel his nearness?

King David must have liked thunderstorms too! As I read Psalm 29 I can imagine David watching a big storm form out over the sea to the far west of his palace. He saw the black, rolling clouds and streaks of lightning as the storm moved closer. When lightning flashed around him and thunder shook the palace, David sat on the patio singing: "The God of glory thunders, the LORD thunders over the mighty waters" (Psalm 29:3). *Read Psalm 29.*

1. This psalm was sung or recited in the public worship of Israel. What style, tone or instrumentation do you think was used when it was sung?

2. What does David want the worshipers to do or feel as they hear or sing this psalm?

How does that compare with your typical approach or response to worship songs on a Sunday morning?

3. Underline the name "LORD" every time it appears. Then circle the name "God of glory" in verse 3. God's glory is the sum of all that God is. What aspects of God's character are revealed in this psalm?

What does it mean that God is the "God of glory"?

---

4. Storms send nature into uproar and turmoil, but David wants the people to give God praise for ruling over the storm. How do you normally respond when storms blow through your life—with turmoil or with praise?

Why do you think you respond that way?

---

5. Psalm 29 is a direct put-down of the Canaanite god Baal (pronounced "bale"). He was worshiped as the god of thunder and rain and as the source of fertility. The Canaanites prayed to Baal for rain when the land was parched and for a stop to the rain when the land was flooded. He was the source of peace in life's struggles. What "gods" does our culture promote as sources of peace in life's storms?

---

6. David wanted God's people to understand that the LORD was the one in charge of storms, not Baal. Describe the peace that can come to you or to a friend when God is recognized as the one in control of life's storms.

7. When we are in a storm, we usually ask God to end the storm or to remove us from the storm. How might we pray differently in light of what is revealed about God in Psalm 29?

---

8. David refers to "the voice of the LORD" seven times (vv. 3-5, 7-9). How can you hear the voice of the LORD in your life?

---

9. According to verses 3-9, what kinds of effects can the LORD's voice have as we listen to him?

---

10. What does God promise to do if we give him the glory and adoration that are appropriate to his majesty (vv. 10-11)?

Pray Psalm 29 back to God. Stand or kneel in his presence and read the psalm as the passionate expression of your joyful heart to him.

Now or Later

Praise psalms (like Psalm 29) are wonderful additions to congregational or small group worship. A few suggestions might help bring these expressions of adoration more alive:

• Enter into the emotion of the psalm by reading it out loud with enthusiasm—reverently but with zeal and passion.

- Memorize the psalm. Then stand and lift your hands in honor and adoration to God as you speak it.

- Be creative. Speak the psalm with others, using alternating voices to give expression to the joy and wonder expressed in the psalm.

- Use the theme of Psalm 29 to write a song or a new psalm to God. He delights in our fresh expressions of praise.

8

The Sovereign God

Sleep therapists tell us that we dream every night. It's often only the weird or dramatic or frightening ones we remember the next day.

The Old Testament prophet Daniel had a whopper of a dream one night—and he remembered every detail the next morning. The dream revolved around four great beasts that emerged from a storm-tossed sea. Each beast was more fearsome than the one before. No one and nothing seemed capable of controlling their violent attacks.

Then Daniel saw something even more astonishing, something that changed his whole perspective: the sovereign God of the universe on a flaming throne, taking his place of judgment. Instead of a whole world out of control, Daniel saw a powerful God in perfect control.

GROUP DISCUSSION. What situations or events prompt you to wonder where God is or if God is really in control?

PERSONAL REFLECTION. Think about a transforming event in your spiritual walk or in your understanding of God. What prompted that sudden change in perspective? What has that transformation produced in your life?

The last beast Daniel saw was the most terrifying of the four—
and the one that triggered the unveiling of the God who rules
our universe in power and authority. *Read Daniel 7:7-14.*

1. Trace the cycle of emotional responses that Daniel would
have experienced during this dream. What would he have felt
at each stage?

2. What do you think the fourth beast in Daniel's vision represents—a person, a nation, a political ideology? Explain how
you've come to that conclusion.

What do you think the "little horn" (v. 8) represents (a person,
nation or ideology)? Why do you think that?

3. Look back through the text and circle the references to the
"Ancient of Days." What aspects of God's character come to
mind when you hear him called the "Ancient of Days"?

4. What does each aspect of Daniel's description of God tell you
about who God is or what God is like?

    clothing:

    hair:

throne:

attendants:

---

5. In a scene revealing God's sovereign authority we are told that "the books were opened" (v. 10). What does that statement convey about human responsibility before God?

---

6. The fourth beast and the little horn are destroyed by God. Can you draw any conclusions from that event about the future of human earthly governments? Explain.

---

7. A new kingdom replaces the destroyed kingdoms of earth. How would you describe this kingdom (vv. 13-14)?

---

8. Have you had experiences that have given you a taste of this kingdom? If so, explain.

Using your imagination, brainstorm what it would be like to live in a kingdom where all of the aspects described here are true all of the time.

9. Jesus used Daniel 7:13 to reveal himself as the divine "son of man" who would return some day in power and majesty to establish God's kingdom (Matthew 26:64). How does Daniel's picture of the son of man expand the normal view of Jesus that is embraced by our society and culture?

---

10. What is the appropriate response in your heart and life to the vision of God in this passage?

---

11. What steps can you take to remind yourself in times of doubt or worry of the authority of God to rule and overrule in our world?

Ask God to give you a new awareness of and appreciation for his sovereign reign in your life. Submit yourself in a fresh way to Jesus as your true King.

Now or Later

Psalm 145 is a song of praise to God the King. Read the psalm, marking the aspects of God's character that are mentioned as you go. Then read the psalm again as an expression of your own praise and honor to your King.

Leader's Notes

MY GRACE IS SUFFICIENT FOR YOU. (2 COR 12:9)

Leading a Bible discussion can be an enjoyable and rewarding experience. But it can also be *scary*—especially if you've never done it before. If this is your feeling, you're in good company. When God asked Moses to lead the Israelites out of Egypt, he replied, "O Lord, please send someone else to do it!" (Ex 4:13). It was the same with Solomon, Jeremiah and Timothy, but God helped these people in spite of their weaknesses, and he will help you as well.

You don't need to be an expert on the Bible or a trained teacher to lead a Bible discussion. The idea behind these inductive studies is that the leader guides group members to discover for themselves what the Bible has to say. This method of learning will allow group members to remember much more of what is said than a lecture would.

These studies are designed to be led easily. As a matter of fact, the flow of questions through the passage from observation to interpretation to application is so natural that you may feel that the studies lead themselves. This study guide is also flexible. You can use it with a variety of groups—student, professional, neighborhood or church groups. Each study takes forty-five to sixty minutes in a group setting.

There are some important facts to know about group dynamics and encouraging discussion. The suggestions listed below should enable you to effectively and enjoyably fulfill your role as leader.

Preparing for the Study

1. Ask God to help you understand and apply the passage in your own life. Unless this happens, you will not be prepared to lead others. Pray too for the various members of the group. Ask God to open your hearts to the message of his Word and motivate you to action.

2. Read the introduction to the entire guide to get an overview of the entire book and the issues which will be explored.

3. As you begin each study, read and reread the assigned Bible passage to familiarize yourself with it.

4. This study guide is based on the New International Version of the Bible. It will help you and the group if you use this translation as the basis for your study and discussion.

5. Carefully work through each question in the study. Spend time in meditation and reflection as you consider how to respond.

6. Write your thoughts and responses in the space provided in the study guide. This will help you to express your understanding of the passage clearly.

7. It might help to have a Bible dictionary handy. Use it to look up any unfamiliar words, names or places. (For additional help on how to study a passage, see chapter five of *How to Lead a LifeGuide Bible Study,* Inter-Varsity Press.)

8. Consider how you can apply the Scripture to your life. Remember that the group will follow your lead in responding to the studies. They will not go any deeper than you do.

9. Once you have finished your own study of the passage, familiarize yourself with the leader's notes for the study you are leading. These are designed to help you in several ways. First, they tell you the purpose the study guide author had in mind when writing the study. Take time to think through how the study questions work together to accomplish that purpose. Second, the notes provide you with additional background information or suggestions on group dynamics for various questions. This information can be useful when people have difficulty understanding or answering a question. Third, the leader's notes can alert you to potential problems you may encounter during the study.

10. If you wish to remind yourself of anything mentioned in the leader's notes, make a note to yourself below that question in the study.

Leading the Study

1. Begin the study on time. Open with prayer, asking God to help the group to understand and apply the passage.

2. Be sure that everyone in your group has a study guide. Encourage the group to prepare beforehand for each discussion by reading the introduction to the guide and by working through the questions in the study.

3. At the beginning of your first time together, explain that these studies are meant to be discussions, not lectures. Encourage the members of the group to participate. However, do not put pressure on those who may be hesitant to speak during the first few sessions. You may want to suggest the following guidelines to your group.

☐ Stick to the topic being discussed.

☐ Your responses should be based on the verses which are the focus of the discussion and not on outside authorities such as commentaries or speakers.

☐ These studies focus on a particular passage of Scripture. Only rarely should you refer to other portions of the Bible. This allows for everyone to participate in in-depth study on equal ground.

☐ Anything said in the group is considered confidential and will not be discussed outside the group unless specific permission is given to do so.

☐ We will listen attentively to each other and provide time for each person present to talk.

☐ We will pray for each other.

4. Have a group member read the introduction at the beginning of the discussion.

5. Every session begins with a group discussion question. The question or activity is meant to be used before the passage is read. The question introduces the theme of the study and encourages group members to begin to open up. Encourage as many members as possible to participate, and be ready to get the discussion going with your own response.

This section is designed to reveal where our thoughts or feelings need to be transformed by Scripture. That is why it is especially important not to read the passage before the discussion question is asked. The passage will tend to color the honest reactions people would otherwise give because they are, of course, supposed to think the way the Bible does.

You may want to supplement the group discussion question with an icebreaker to help people to get comfortable. See the community section of *Small Group Idea Book* for more ideas.

You also might want to use the personal reflection question with your group. Either allow a time of silence for people to respond individually or discuss it together.

6. Have a group member (or members if the passage is long) read aloud the passage to be studied. Then give people several minutes to read the passage again silently so that they can take it all in.

7. Question 1 will generally be an overview question designed to briefly survey the passage. Encourage the group to look at the whole passage, but try to avoid getting sidetracked by questions or issues that will be addressed later in the study.

8. As you ask the questions, keep in mind that they are designed to be used just as they are written. You may simply read them aloud. Or you may prefer to express them in your own words.

There may be times when it is appropriate to deviate from the study guide. For example, a question may have already been answered. If so, move on to the next question. Or someone may raise an important question not covered in the guide. Take time to discuss it, but try to keep the group from going off on tangents.

9. Avoid answering your own questions. If necessary, repeat or re-phrase them until they are clearly understood. Or point out something you read in the leader's notes to clarify the context or meaning. An eager group quickly becomes passive and silent if they think the leader will do most of the talking.

10. Don't be afraid of silence. People may need time to think about the question before formulating their answers.

11. Don't be content with just one answer. Ask, "What do the rest of you think?" or "Anything else?" until several people have given answers to the question.

12. Acknowledge all contributions. Try to be affirming whenever possible. Never reject an answer. If it is clearly off-base, ask, "Which verse led you to that conclusion?" or again, "What do the rest of you think?"

13. Don't expect every answer to be addressed to you, even though this will probably happen at first. As group members become more at ease, they will begin to truly interact with each other. This is one sign of healthy discussion.

14. Don't be afraid of controversy. It can be very stimulating. If you don't resolve an issue completely, don't be frustrated. Move on and keep it in mind for later. A subsequent study may solve the problem.

15. Periodically summarize what the group has said about the passage. This helps to draw together the various ideas mentioned and gives continuity to the study. But don't preach.

16. At the end of the Bible discussion you may want to allow group members a time of quiet to work on an idea under "Now or Later." Then discuss what you experienced. Or you may want to encourage group members to work on these ideas between meetings. Give an opportunity

during the session for people to talk about what they are learning.

17. Conclude your time together with conversational prayer, adapting the prayer suggestion at the end of the study to your group. Ask for God's help in following through on the commitments you've made.

18. End on time.

Many more suggestions and helps are found in *How to Lead a LifeGuide Bible Study*.

Components of Small Groups

A healthy small group should do more than study the Bible. There are four components to consider as you structure your time together.

Nurture. Small groups help us to grow in our knowledge and love of God. Bible study is the key to making this happen and is the foundation of your small group.

Community. Small groups are a great place to develop deep friendships with other Christians. Allow time for informal interaction before and after each study. Plan activities and games that will help you get to know each other. Spend time having fun together going on a picnic or cooking dinner together.

Worship and prayer. Your study will be enhanced by spending time praising God together in prayer or song. Pray for each other's needs and keep track of how God is answering prayer in your group. Ask God to help you to apply what you are learning in your study.

Outreach. Reaching out to others can be a practical way of applying what you are learning, and it will keep your group from becoming self-focused. Host a series of evangelistic discussions for your friends or neighbors. Clean up the yard of an elderly friend. Serve at a soup kitchen together, or spend a day working on a Habitat house.

Many more suggestions and helps in each of these areas are found in *Small Group Idea Book*. Information on building a small group can be found in *Small Group Leaders' Handbook* and *The Big Book on Small Groups* (both from InterVarsity Press). Reading through one of these books would be worth your time.

Study 1. One Supreme Being. Genesis 1.

Purpose: To encounter God as the Creator and Sustainer of life and to respond appropriately to him.

Group discussion. The purpose of this question is to get the members of the group to think seriously about why they believe God exists. It is not designed to stir up a lengthy debate about whether each answer is a valid proof. Allow members to share their responses freely and then move on to the study.

A question may be raised about the "gender" of references to God. The reality is that God is neither male nor female, but is pure spirit. The Bible, however, consistently refers to God as "he." Most of the images of God in Scripture are also male; "Father" comes to mind, for example. In this guide, I have followed the biblical example and refer to God as "he" or "him."

Question 1. God is active throughout this account: he speaks (vv. 3, 6, 9, 11, 14, 20, 22, 24, 26, 28, 29), he makes and creates (vv. 1, 7, 16, 21, 25, 27, 31), he sees (vv. 4, 10, 12, 18, 21, 25, 31), he names (vv. 5, 8, 10), he reasons within himself (v. 26), he blesses animals and humans (vv. 22, 28), and he commands and instructs humans (vv. 28-30). God personally relates to his creation.

Question 2. God forms and fills the earth primarily as a dwelling place for human beings. His human creatures were the final piece, the crown of his creation. God did not create humans simply to do his work (the view of most pagan mythologies). Instead God gave human beings the place of honor and glory as rulers and stewards of his creation (Ps 8:5-8).

Question 3. The Old Testament Scriptures were originally written in the Hebrew language. The names and titles of God that appear in our Bibles are therefore translations of Hebrew words. *Elohim* is actually a plural form of the word *El,* which means "first," and came to refer to God as the Supreme Being over all creation. The plural form may have been used to intensify the majesty of God, or because it hints of plurality in God—Father, Son and Spirit. The verb "created" in verse 1 is singular in form, though, demonstrating that God was thought of as one being. The Bible is characteristically monotheistic in outlook—there is only one God.

The writer of Hebrews says that "the universe was formed at God's command, so that what is seen was not made out of what was visible" (11:3). The Christian grasps this truth "by faith." Again, be careful that the study does not become a debate on *how* God created. The focus should be on God's power and God's supremacy. If he can simply speak a word of command and bring stars or trees or animals into existence, he is a God of limitless power.

Question 5. At the end of each day God declares his creation "good"—and then, at the end of the sixth day, he looks at the totality of creation and sees that it is all "very good" (v. 31). God is not the source of evil or imperfection. There is no moral darkness in God at all (1 Jn 1:5). The original creation came from the pure work of God's hands.

Since the created world before the entrance of sin was good, we as God's creatures—and certainly now as God's redeemed creatures—should respect and honor God's world that has been entrusted to us.

Question 6. God appoints Adam and Eve as stewards of his creation. God created the earth as a dwelling place for humans, and he gives them authority to subdue the earth in order to provide for their needs. We are to act, however, as caretakers of what does not ultimately belong to us. It is ours to use but not to destroy.

Christians have taken a wide range of positions on the issue of "creation care," but all agree that we have a responsibility to treat the earth as God's property rather than as our own. The fact that Adam and Eve were made "in the image of God" (v. 27) implies that God expects human beings to use the earth and its resources wisely. We are to govern the earth with the same sense of responsibility that God exercises in creating and caring for the universe.

Question 7. Interpreters of the Bible have debated extensively what it means for humans to be created in the image of God. Some believe it means that we *represent* God as the rulers over creation. Others believe the image of God is revealed in the *relationships* human beings can have with God and with each other—relationships based on love and commitment. Still other interpreters see *resemblances* between God and humans such as the capacity for reason, morality and a sense of creativity. The fullness of the image of God probably lies in all these facets. Human beings are unique creatures, not just the highest branch on the evolutionary tree. Even though sin has clouded the glory of the image of God in us, the image still remains (Jas 3:9). Our respect for human life in all its stages stems from an acknowledgment of God's image within every human being.

Question 8. The existence of a powerful, sovereign God who made us and who is concerned for our welfare should prompt several responses in us: adoration and worship, obedience to his commands, respect and gratitude for his many gifts, and a sense of responsibility to do what honors and pleases him. Maybe you can write the various responses on a white board or poster board and then list under each some practical ways to work those responses into daily life. We can respond to God with gratitude, for example, by being more intentional in thanking God for his provision and gifts each day—thanking him specifically for food or rest or shelter or health.

Now or Later. Reading Psalm 8 as a closing "prayer" will reinforce a sense of God's majesty and his personal concern for his human creatures.

Study 2. God Most High. Genesis 14:17-24.
Purpose: To explore what it means to serve and trust God Most High in the contemporary world.
Question 1. You will get helpful background for this study if you read the entire fourteenth chapter of Genesis. Questions to ask Abram (his name was not changed to Abraham until Genesis 17:5) might be: How were you able to defeat such a powerful coalition of kings with only 318 men? Did you know Melchizedek before this event? Why did you give Melchizedek a tenth of the spoils; why not half—or none?

Questions for Melchizedek might be: Who are you anyway? How did you come to know and follow the true God? What qualifies you to be a priest? What did you do with the tenth of all the goods that Abram gave you?
Question 2. Melchizedek (whose name in Hebrew means "king of righteousness") is called the king of Salem (most likely a shortened form of the word *Jerusalem*). He provided a meal for the victorious army as a sign of friendship and hospitality. The meal of bread and wine here is not connected in any way to the New Testament Communion meal or Eucharist.

Melchizedek is also called a "priest of God Most High." He was a believer in the one true God and functioned as a priest in his blessing of Abram. The blessing attributes Abram's victory to the power of God. Melchizedek also functioned as a priest when he received Abram's gift of one-tenth (a "tithe") of the recaptured possessions. The New Testament book of Hebrews presents Jesus as a priest "in the order of Melchizedek" (Heb 5:5-10; 6:20–7:17).
Question 3. "God Most High" in Hebrew is *El Elyon*. The name *El* (the basis for *Elohim* in study one) was the common Hebrew term for "God." To that name is added the attribute *Elyon*, meaning "most high" or "most exalted." The name acknowledges God's place as Ruler and King over all and God's authority and power as the highest being in the universe. Nations and tribes may have their own gods, but the true God is exalted over all.
Question 4. This question is designed to bring our trust in God's power and authority into the day-to-day operation of our lives. We may say that we believe in a powerful God, but are we resting and relying on his power in our relationships and on the job, or are we trying to be the ones in control? God had promised Abram, for example, that he and his descen-

dants would possess the land of Canaan, but Abram refused to use military force to accomplish that promise. He would not take any of the spoils for himself either. He didn't want to claim any part of the honor that was due to God alone.

Question 5. Abram gave a gift to God through God's authorized representative, Melchizedek the priest. The tenth (the tithe) was the victor's share and therefore could have been claimed by Abram. By giving it to Melchizedek, Abram was acknowledging that God's power was the true source of his victory over the enemy kings. He was also affirming the truth of Melchizedek's words in verses 19 and 20. Abram's action is the basis for the later Israelite and Christian practice of tithing (regularly giving one-tenth of our income to the Lord through his representatives—priests in Israel and church leaders today). Generous, sacrificial giving is one way to acknowledge God's lordship over all we possess.

Questions 6-7. Abram did not want the king of Sodom to claim any part of his success. Rather, Abram wanted the glory to go to God Most High alone.

It seems likely that Abram swore the oath to God before he pursued the kings, as a commitment before the battle to honor God fully in the battle. Abram was depending on God, not human benefactors or their gifts, to become a "great nation" (Gen 12:2).

It is significant that Abram calls God "the LORD, God Most High, Creator of heaven and earth" (v. 22). He makes it clear that *Elohim, El Elyon* and *Yahweh*, which means "the LORD" (see study 3), are one and the same. Abram was not a believer in many gods with many names, but a follower of the one true God who had several significant names.

Question 8. Abram made the oath as an expression of his deep trust in and devotion to the LORD. He honored God by giving God praise for his successes, by giving God a gift, and by being a witness to God's power and blessing. These are all ways we can serve and demonstrate our trust in God Most High.

Question 9. Abram may have emerged from this experience with a new level of trust in God and in God's promises. It may have also stirred new courage in him to follow the LORD completely, and a new sensitivity to giving God the honor and gratitude he deserves.

Question 10. You might want to use a white board or poster board to list the appropriate responses to God Most High and then to write the group's suggestions for incorporating those responses into their worship and routine activities.

Study 3. God's Personal Name. Psalm 68:1-20.

Purpose: To investigate the meaning of God's personal, covenant name and to deepen our response of worship to him.

Introduction. It might help you as a leader to read 2 Samuel 6 as background for this psalm. We don't know with certainty that the historical setting of Psalm 68 was David's transport of the ark of the covenant into Jerusalem, but the psalm fits the scene very well. Verse 1 of the psalm echoes Numbers 10:35—words spoken by Moses when the ark was moved in the wilderness hundreds of years earlier.

The ark of the covenant was a gold-covered box that rested in the inner sanctuary of Israel's worship center. It was a reminder to the people of God's faithfulness to his promises and his presence with them. David's desire was to build a permanent place for Israel's worship in the city of Jerusalem. God allowed him to collect material for the temple, but it was his son Solomon who built the final structure.

Questions 1-2. David's poetic review of God's care for his people over the centuries was designed to stir Israel's faith and confidence in God's continuing care. God did wonderful things in the past—and God is the same today. He is willing and able to help us. He still dwells among his people in sovereign authority. His name and character and power are the same.

Question 3. Some members of the group may not be able to point to a specific work of God in their lives. Remind them of their deliverance from the grip of sin and death when they came to believe in Jesus as Savior. Ask them to recall times when God protected them or provided for them. Even if a member of your group is not a Christian, God's work has brought them into your group so he can reveal himself more fully to them through the study of the Bible.

Question 4. The name *Yahweh* ("LORD") comes from a form of the Hebrew verb for "to be." The name suggests several things about God: (1) God is self-existent—he does not need anything or anyone outside himself; (2) God is unchanging in his character—he is not in the process of becoming something different from what he is; and (3) God is eternal—he exists and has existed forever.

The fullest revelation of God's covenant name came to Moses when God spoke to him from the burning bush. When Moses asked God his name, God said, "I AM WHO I AM [Yahweh]. This is what you are to say to the Israelites: 'I AM has sent me to you'" (Ex 3:13-15). In the New Testament, Jesus is called "Lord" (Greek: *kurios*), identifying Jesus as the God of the Old Testament, the same God who had revealed himself to Moses. On several occasions Jesus referred to himself as the "I am" (Jn 6:35; 8:12; 14:6; 18:5-6), and in doing so he drew his listeners (and the readers of John's Gospel) back to God's revelation of himself to Moses as the "I AM."

The aspects of God's character that David focuses on are God's compassion and care for the weakest and most vulnerable of his people—orphans, widows, the lonely, prisoners. If God cares so deeply for those in our culture who have the least in terms of resources or options, he will also care for those who have more but who are willing to rely on him. Listen carefully as members share their own response to God's character. They may reveal areas in their lives where they are struggling and need help or encouragement.

Question 6. God may choose to work in power and provide dramatic answers to prayer—or God may choose to work quietly through what appear to be ordinary means. A believer who is sick may be raised up in a miraculous healing or through the longer process of medical care and rest. Both routes are expressions of God's power and God's care, and both are worthy of praise to him.

Question 7. Holy angels are powerful agents of God's activity in the world. We are not usually aware of their ministry to us, but they actively "serve those who will inherit salvation" (Heb 1:14). Angels minister to God's people in external ways like protection, direction, provision; the Holy Spirit ministers to us internally. If the group has an interest in what the Bible teaches about angels, consider using the *Angels* LifeGuide study in the future.

Questions 8-9. Verse 19 is translated differently in older versions of the Bible. The King James or Authorized Version says: "Blessed be the Lord, who daily loadeth us with benefits." The idea is that God loads good things on us. Most modern versions translate the verse to mean that God takes the load of cares and concerns from us. The person burdened with problems or difficult circumstances needs to hear not only that the Lord can help but also that he is willing at any time to help lift the weight of those concerns from us.

In verse 20 David adds that those who follow the LORD will "escape from death." Old Testament believers knew very little about what lay beyond death's door. They were confident, however, that the LORD who had cared for them so abundantly in life would not abandon them in the life beyond. We as New Testament believers have the assurance that, when our spirit leaves this body in death, we will be present with the Lord (2 Cor 5:8). Death no longer holds us in its fearful grip. We also know that one generation of believers will escape death in the rapture when Jesus returns for his people and removes them from this world (1 Thess 4:13-18).

Question 10. The name Yahweh points to God as the eternal, self-existent LORD of all. He does not need us; we need him. But this psalm makes clear that the LORD uses his power, not to force us down in fearful submission but to care for us as his own dear children. He is a God we can trust and serve with joyful, thankful hearts.

Study 4. The God Who Provides. Genesis 22:1-14.

Purpose: To discover God's ability to provide what we need even when we think all hope is lost.

Group discussion. Be sensitive to the responses from the group. If someone shares a particularly deep or recent experience, you may want to say a brief prayer for that person before going on. You'll also want to ask just one or two to respond so the discussion stays focused and so you have time to concentrate on the study questions.

Question 1. Christians have been troubled about several aspects of this account. Why would God ask Abraham to do such a thing in the first place? Isn't this against God's moral law? Why did Abraham agree to do it—and apparently without any protest? Why did Isaac submit? Isaac was not a boy but a young man who could easily have overpowered his one-hundred-plus-year-old father. And what about Sarah—was she told? Hopefully the questions raised will prompt the group to think more deeply about this well-known passage than they have in the past.

Question 2. Abraham's prompt obedience is an indication of his confident trust in God. He may have had some theories about how God could still fulfill his promises if Isaac was slain, but in the end Abraham was willing to trust God during a very difficult time.

Question 3. Some group members may not see any present problems in their lives as tests from God. Explain that God may use any of the various trials of life as opportunities to put our faith or wisdom or patience to the test. God allows the difficulty to come and then carefully observes how we respond.

Testing should be distinguished from tempting someone toward evil. God does not tempt anyone (Jas 1:13). He does, however, place us in situations that test our commitment and trust in him.

Question 4. You may hear differing opinions as the answers to this question are given, but it seems clear that Abraham's full intention was to kill Isaac. He believed that God would bring good to him and glory to himself from this situation, even if Isaac died.

Question 5. Abraham said with confidence that both he and Isaac would return to them ("*we* will come back"). The writer of the book of Hebrews says that Abraham believed God would raise Isaac from the dead (Heb 11:17-19).

Question 7. Abraham wanted his descendants (physical and spiritual) and everyone who came to this place in the land of Israel to grasp the gracious character of the Lord. God in grace provided a substitute to fulfill the requirement that God had placed on Abraham. Abraham knew this aspect of God's character even before he raised the knife to slay his son. When Isaac asked, "Where is the lamb?" Abraham's response was, "God himself will provide" (vv. 7-8). In the same way, God will provide for us. He stands ready and willing to supply grace in any circumstance (2 Cor 12:9). God's greatest provision toward us was the giving of his own Son, Jesus, as our substitute on the cross. We had nothing to offer God that would make us right before him. Jesus, through his own sacrifice, provided us with a right standing before God.

Questions 8-9. These questions will likely prompt a very personal response, and some in the group may find it difficult to give their answer. You as the leader may want to share first. Vulnerability on your part will give others in the group the courage to share their responses. One way to end the study is to construct a small "altar"—a stack of books will work—and then give each member a piece of paper on which they can write what their "Isaac" is. Then fold the papers and place them "on the altar" as an act of submission to God. In doing this, confidentiality is preserved, but each person has the opportunity to offer their sacrifice to God in their own hearts.

Now or Later. Many students of the Bible see the principle of substitutionary atonement introduced in Scripture at this point. The lamb died in the place of Isaac. Later in the biblical story, Jesus would die on the cross in the place of sinners. The penalty of sin was paid but not by us. God himself took our place and paid the penalty his justice demanded.

Study 5. The LORD Almighty. 1 Samuel 17:1-51.

Purpose: To challenge us toward greater confidence in God's ability and willingness to work powerfully in our lives.

Question 1. The author of 1 Samuel goes to great lengths to paint a sobering picture of Goliath. Goliath's armor was the finest produced at this time in history. Most of his armaments were bronze, including a long coat of interlocking plates that weighed 125 pounds. The spearhead was a fifteen-pound missile of iron. Put all that armor on a nine-and-a-half-foot body builder and you have one intimidating champion!

The ancient Greeks (to whom the Philistines were distantly related) sometimes decided issues of war by sending out two champions to fight between the battle lines. The winner's side would claim the victory. King Saul (who stood a head taller than any of his men according to 1 Samuel 9:2) should have been Israel's champion, but he was filled with fear and a lack of faith (1 Sam 17:11).

Questions 2-3. Saul tried to motivate his soldiers to fight Goliath with promises of money and the hand of his daughter in marriage. In addition, the entire household (extended family) of the soldier's father would be exempt from taxes.

It seems at first glance (vv. 26-27) that David was enticed by these offers, but his true motive becomes clear as the story unfolds. He fought Goliath to defend the honor of God's name.

Question 5. The Bible's declaration that God is all-powerful means that God never enters a situation that he is unable to change. He is never afraid or helpless. He is never powerless to come to our aid. In fact, God is always able to do beyond what we ask or imagine as we trust him to help us.

The descriptive title "the LORD Almighty" is literally "the LORD of hosts" and is used more than 250 times in the Old Testament. The word *hosts* referred to any group, human or angelic, called to do the bidding of the God of Israel. The idea is that God has infinite resources at his disposal to accomplish all that he desires.

Question 7. The fears we experience as we face adversaries can be met with the power of God. David came against Goliath with confidence in the LORD Almighty. We may not see those enemies defeated in one encounter, but we can be assured that God is ready and able to stand with us each time we come against our spiritual foes.

Question 8. David's prediction of Goliath's defeat did not rest on his skills or abilities but on his trust in God. David knew that Goliath's defeat was the will of God because of Goliath's mockery of God's character and his dishonor toward God's people. David just wanted to be a willing instrument in God's hand.